First Facts®

The Solar System

Space Probes

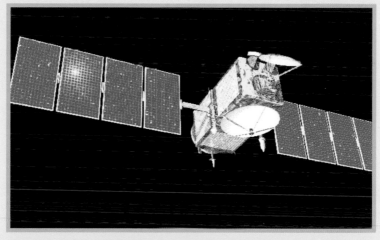

by Steve Kortenkamp

Consultant:
James Gerard
Aerospace Education Specialist, NASA
Kennedy Space Center, Florida

Capstone
press®

Mankato, Minnesota

First Facts is published by Capstone Press,
151 Good Counsel Drive, P.O. Box 669, Mankato, Minnesota 56002.
www.capstonepress.com

Library of Congress Cataloging-in-Publication Data
Kortenkamp, Steve.
    Space probes / by Steve Kortenkamp.
    p. cm.—(First facts. The solar system)
    Summary: "Describes what space probes are, history of space probes, and discoveries made
by using probes"—Provided by publisher.
    Includes bibliographical references and index.
    ISBN-13: 978-1-4296-0063-7 (hardcover)
    ISBN-10: 1-4296-0063-2 (hardcover)
    1. Space probes—Juvenile literature. 2. Outer space—Exploration—Juvenile literature. I. Title.
II. Series.
TL795.3.K667 2008
629.43'5—dc22   2006100064

Editorial Credits
Jennifer Besel, editor; Juliette Peters, set designer; Patrick D. Dentinger, book designer; Jo Miller,
    photo researcher

Photo Credits
Astronomical Society of the Pacific/NASA, 14–15
NASA, 1; Marshall Space Flight Center, 8; Johns Hopkins University Applied Physics
    Laboratory/Southwest Research Institute, 18–19; JPL, cover, 4–5, 6–7, 9, 10–11, 12–13, 16, 21;
    JPL/Caltech, 20; JPL/UMD, 17

1 2 3 4 5 6 12 11 10 09 08 07

Table of Contents

Robots in Space

Did you know scientists use robots to explore space? These robots are called space probes. Probes are **spacecraft** that can go places that people can't. They can explore the hot planet Mercury or frozen worlds far out in space.

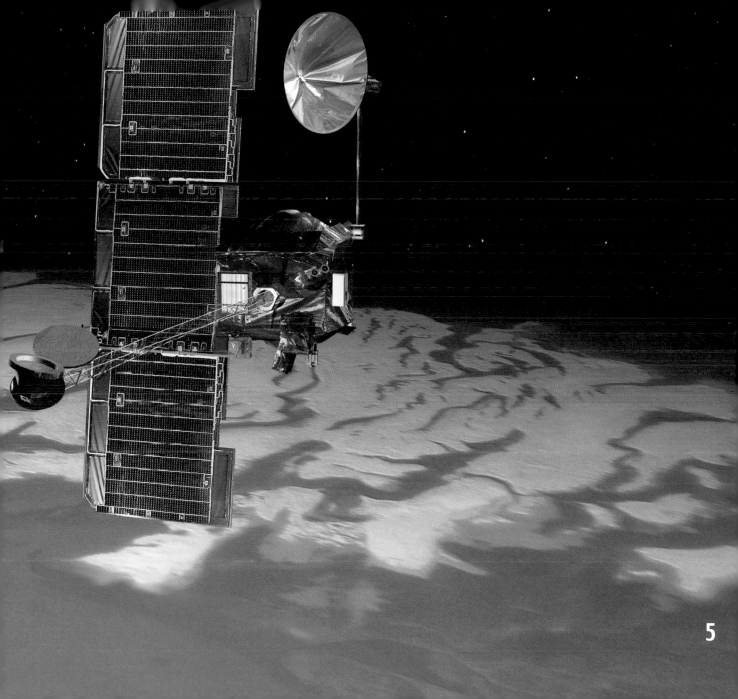

How Probes Explore Space

Not all space probes are the same. **Satellites** circle an object and study it from space. **Landers** touch down on an object. **Rovers** land on an object too. But rovers can drive around. Landers can't.

Probes take pictures and gather information. Then they send all the information back to scientists on Earth.

Spirit Mars rover

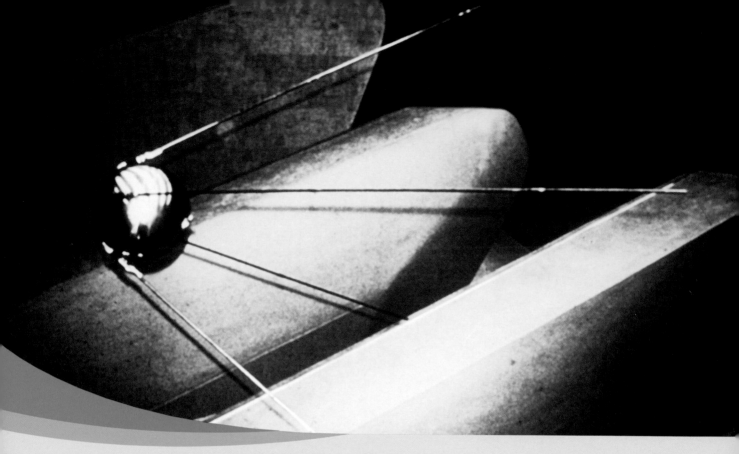

The First Space Probes

The first space probes didn't go very far into space. *Sputnik* was the first probe. Russian scientists used this satellite to study Earth.

The first probes were also very simple. The United States' *Explorer 1* only had thermometers and a tool to study **radiation**.

Probes to the Moon

As rocket science improved, scientists sent probes farther into space. Their next stop was the Moon. The probes took pictures and landed on the Moon. Astronauts used the pictures to find safe places to land when they went to the Moon.

Fun Fact!

The first Moon probes didn't have landing gear. They crashed on purpose so scientists could get really close-up pictures.

Ranger 9 Moon probe

Exploring Other Planets

Space probes have been sent all around the solar system. Almost everything we know about the planets we learned from probes.

When scientists sent probes to Venus, they found volcanoes and lightning there. The *Mars Odyssey* probe showed scientists that Mars is a dry desert planet.

! Fun Fact!
Space probes have visited every planet in our solar system.

Mars Odyssey space probe

Neptune's moon Triton

The most famous space probes are *Voyager 1* and 2. They explored the giant planets Jupiter, Saturn, Uranus, and Neptune.

When *Voyager 2* flew past Neptune, scientists were able to see its icy moon Triton. They saw gas and dust shooting out of holes in the ground.

! Fun Fact!
Scientists used the *Voyager* probes to discover new moons and rings going around all four giant planets.

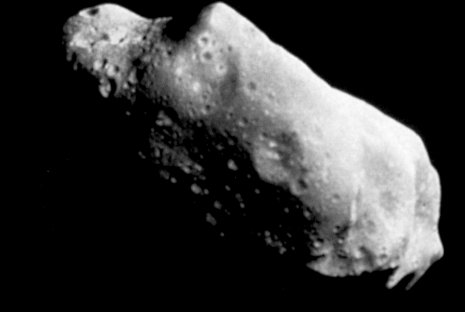

asteroid Ida with its moon

Asteroids and Comets

Space probes are sent to explore **asteroids** and **comets** too. The *Galileo* probe showed scientists that asteroids can have moons, just like planets.

Scientists crashed the *Deep Impact* probe into a comet. Dust and gases flew out. Scientists learned that comets are fluffy, like frozen cotton balls.

Future Discoveries

Scientists usually wait years for probes to get to their targets. The *New Horizons* probe is on its way to Pluto. It will get there in 2015. And the *Voyager* probes are now far past all the planets. Who knows what new worlds they will show us out there.

Fun Fact!
The *Voyager* probes have been exploring space for almost 30 years. They have enough power to keep going for another 20 years.

New Horizons space probe

Modern space probes are very complex machines. Some of them even carry smaller probes. The *Cassini* probe is circling Saturn and exploring its rings and moons. *Cassini* dropped a mini-probe on Saturn's giant moon Titan. Pictures from this lander showed rivers and lakes on the surface of Titan.

Think Big!

All space probes get their start with a question. Scientists ask questions like, "What's on the inside of a comet?" Then they make a plan for how to answer the question with a space probe. Do you have a question about the solar system? How could you use a space probe to answer your question?

Glossary

asteroid (AS-tuh-roid)—a large space rock that moves around the Sun; asteroids are too small to be called planets.

comet (KOM-it)—a ball of rock and ice that circles the Sun

lander (LAND-uhr)—a spacecraft that lands on an object to study the surface

radiation (ray-dee-AY-shuhn)—rays of energy given off by certain elements

rover (ROH-vur)—a small vehicle that people can move by using remote control; rovers are used to explore objects in space.

satellite (SAT-uh-lite)—a spacecraft that circles Earth; satellites take pictures and send messages to Earth.

spacecraft (SPAYSS-kraft)—a vehicle that travels in space

Read More

Angelo, Joseph A. *Robot Spacecraft*. Frontiers in Space. New York: Facts on File, 2007.

Asimov, Isaac. *Exploring Outer Space*. Isaac Asimov's 21st Century Library of the Universe. Past and Present. Milwaukee: Gareth Stevens, 2006.

Kerrod, Robin. *Space Probes*. The History of Space Exploration. Milwaukee: World Almanac Library, 2005.

Internet Sites

FactHound offers a safe, fun way to find Internet sites related to this book. All of the sites on FactHound have been researched by our staff.

Here's how:
1. Visit *www.facthound.com*
2. Choose your grade level.
3. Type in this book ID **1429600632** for age-appropriate sites. You may also browse subjects by clicking on letters, or by clicking on pictures and words.
4. Click on the **Fetch It** button.

Facthound will fetch the best sites for you!

Index